DEMONSTRATING GOD'S KINGDOM

The Call of Every Believer

DWAYNE NORMAN

Empyrion Publishing
Broken Arrow OK

Demonstrating God's Kingdom
ISBN: 978-1490496498
Copyright 2013 by Dwayne Norman

Empyrion Press
Broken Arrow Ok
university@rickmanis.com

Unless otherwise indicated, all Scripture quotations are taken
from the New King James Version of the Bible.

TABLE OF CONTENTS

1

GOD'S KINGDOM: IN WORD AND POWER

Trying to intellectually out debate people into getting saved is not good enough in these last days. We <u>must</u> have Kingdom demonstration!! The Apostle Paul said that his speech and his preaching were not with persuasive words of human wisdom, but in demonstration of the Spirit and of power, so that the people's faith would not be in the wisdom of men but in the power of God (I Corinthians 2:4,5;4:20). He also said that the Kingdom of God is not in word but in power, and that the Gospel he preached did not come to the people in word only, but also in power, and in the Holy Spirit and in much assurance, as you know what kind of men we were among you for your sake (I Thessalonians 1:5).

In my book "The Awesome Power in the Message

of the Cross" I spoke of how my brother and I spent about 3 years witnessing for the Lord in the "red light" district of Dallas, Texas back in the late 70's. We were attending Christ for the Nations Bible School as well as operating in what they called the prostitution ministry. Every Friday and Saturday night from 10pm until 2am we would share God's Word with prostitutes, pimps, homosexuals, drug addicts and others who were lost. We spent most of our time talking to the people around one particular store front (plaza) area in the city.

On one end of the plaza was a fast food place, in the middle was a place called the Rap Session (where they modeled negligees) and on the end was the spot light bar. One night my brother (Chris) and I were there handing out tracts and telling people about the Lord when we heard a dog scream. He was hit by a car crossing the four lane road in front of the plaza. I went over to Chris and said that we should go and pray for the dog. He agreed and we walked over to where the dog had been hit. He was laid out in the middle of the road on his stomach, all four legs spread out and blood coming out of his mouth. He looked dead (but we didn't have a stethoscope to confirm it). When we laid hands on his back I couldn't feel any breathing or movement of any kind. If he wasn't dead, he was in very bad shape. When we got out there a group of people had made a circle around the dog and were just staring at him.

Obviously, the cars had to drive around us while we were there. Chris and I bent down over the dog and laid our hands on his back. We prayed in tongues for a couple of minutes then I began to speak to the dog. I said, "Dog, I'm talking to you! I command all of the blood to stop flowing out of your mouth! I command all of your internal organs to be healed and made whole in Jesus' Name!" After just a few minutes of that, the dog jumps up, all by himself, pushing our hands out of the way, totally healed! A man standing in front of us reaches down and picks up the dog. I assumed it belonged to him. I looked at the man and said, "Sir, Jesus just healed your dog!" He said, "thank you for healing my dog, thank you for healing my dog, thank you for healing my dog!" He said it 3 times every time he said it. I responded, "Sir, I did not heal your dog. Jesus healed your dog." Again, he said, "Thank you for healing my dog, thank you for healing my dog, thank you for healing my dog." This time I said, "I didn't heal your dog. Jesus healed him and because He did I would like a few minutes of your time." Well, we had a nice little crowd gathered around us in the middle of this four lane road. I knew that we couldn't stay out there much longer so I quickly opened my Bible to the book of John, chapter 3. The story of Nicodemus, where Jesus told him you must be "born-again" to enter the Kingdom of God. I read the story out loud to all the people gathered on the street. I then asked the man if he believed what I just read. He said, "Thank you for healing my dog, thank you for healing my dog, thank you for healing my dog." I said, "You're welcome, but did you understand what I just read to you?" He said, "Yea I understand, thank you for healing my dog." I knew we couldn't keep blocking traffic any longer, so I said, "Remember that Jesus healed your dog because He's real and alive today!" I then told everybody they could go, but I guarantee you that they left knowing that Jesus is alive!

The crowd we had out there was comprised of prostitutes, pimps, homosexuals, drug addicts, etc..., but they knew how to put 2 and 2 together when they saw this healing-miracle. Try with me, if you can, to imagine what they were thinking when this happened. They saw a dog get hit by a car. He's laid out in the middle of the road and looks dead. Two strangers come by and lay their hands on the "dead dog" and command him to come back to life in Jesus' Name. Now, they're probably thinking, "Man can't heal a dead dog, but the dog jumps up when the Name of Jesus is spoken! The stranger then stands up and says that Jesus is alive! If Jesus wasn't real or just some myth then His Name would have no power, but yet the dog jumped up. It looks like Jesus must be real." Isn't that what happened with the Apostle Paul in Acts

13?

Acts 13:6-12 says:

"Now when they had gone through the island to Paphos, they found a certain sorcerer, a false prophet, a Jew whose name was BarJesus, who was with the proconsul, Sergius Paulus, an intelligent man. This man called for Barnabas and Saul and sought to hear the word of God.

But Elymas the sorcerer (for so his name is translated) withstood them, seeking to turn the proconsul away from the faith.

Then Saul, who also is called Paul, filled with the Holy Spirit, looked intently at him and said, "O full of all deceit and all fraud, you son of the devil, you enemy of all righteousness, will you not cease perverting the straight ways of the Lord?

And now, indeed, the hand of the Lord is upon you, and you shall be blind, not seeing the sun for a time." And immediately a dark mist fell on him, and he went around seeking someone to lead him by the hand.

Then the proconsul believed, when he saw what had been done, being astonished at the teaching of the Lord.

What caused the proconsul to be astonished at the teaching of the Lord? What caused him to believe the message that Saul (also known as Paul) preached to him? It was when that message of the Kingdom of God was demonstrated in power! As a Christian, it's very important that you believe the Bible is true, but that doesn't mean the lost are going to believe, just because you do. Some people will need to see a demonstration of the Spirit and power of God, and did you know that's ok? The Lord wants to prove to people how real He is, but only to those who sincerely want to know.

In Luke chapter 5, Jesus borrowed Peter's boat to have a platform to preach from. When He was through, He told Peter to launch out into the deep for a catch. After hesitating a moment, he threw his nets out and caught a great number of fish. The Bible says in verses 7-9:

"So they signaled to their partners in the other boat to come and help them. And they came and filled both the boats, so that they began to sink.

When Simon Peter saw it, he fell down at Jesus' knees, saying, "Depart from me, for I am a sinful man, O Lord!"

For he and all who were with him were astonished at the catch of fish which they had taken."

Do you see what happened here? Because of this "financial" miracle, Peter came under conviction.

There's a connection between demonstrating God's Kingdom and getting people saved. Jesus didn't give an altar call after their boats were full, but Peter responded as though He did. Peter came under conviction when the power of God was manifested, why? The connection I spoke about is the <u>love</u> of God. The reason the Lord is willing to manifest His power and prove He's real, is because He loves us so much. This is what strongly affected Peter, but God used the boat load of fish to get his attention.

Some time ago, my wife (Leia) and I were ministering in a Sunday morning service in Kentucky. The Lord was healing people and growing out arms and legs. Right in the midst of the healings, a man comes over to me in a wheel chair. I assumed he just wanted to be healed. I was ready for him to tell me what was wrong, when he said that he needed to get right with God. He came under conviction like Peter did when he saw the miracles.

The Lord Jesus said in John 10:37,38:

"If I do not do the works of My Father, do not believe Me;

But if I do, though you do not believe Me, believe the works that you may know and believe that the Father is in Me, and I in Him."

The Lord said that if you don't believe what I said

is true, or if I can't convince you by my preaching, then the works (miracles) I do should prove what I say is true. God will prove Himself real to those who honestly want to know if Jesus is the only way to the Father and Heaven (John 14:6). He may send an angel to them, heal their body or let them see and experience a miracle. God knows what every person needs to convince them that He is the true and only God and that He loves them.

One night Chris and I were not able to park in our usual place. We had to park down a dark road and walk back up to this plaza. On the way there we came upon two homosexuals and began to talk to them about the Lord. One of them was speaking in a "higher tone" voice. I looked him in the eyes and said, "If you let me, I will cast that demon out of you!" He didn't laugh at me, but very seriously said, "Do it!" As soon as I commanded the spirit of homosexuality to come out of him in Jesus' Name his voice dropped to where he sounded like a man again. We led both of them to the Lord that night. I believe they both got saved when they saw the power of God demonstrated.

God's best is for people to believe the Word of God immediately when they hear it, but many won't believe until they see a demonstration that convinces them God's Word is true. Every where Jesus went, He taught and preached the Gospel, healed the sick, cast out demons and worked miracles. Are we doing that in our churches today? Jesus demonstrated what He taught, in the Spirit and power of God among the people! Are we doing that in our churches today? Jesus preached God's Word uncompromisingly (in love) to everyone; even at the risk of losing His own disciples (John 6:60,61). He never sought to please man; not for money, fame or greater attendance in His meetings! Are we operating the same way in our churches today? If we truly fear the Lord then our hearts cry will be to please our Father in all that we say and do, even if we lose people and they quit giving into our ministries. Did God ever let Jesus down? Did Jesus ever run out of people to preach to? Did He ever run out of money? Did He finally have to close His ministry down and go back to being a carpenter? There is nothing wrong with being a carpenter, fireman, teacher, policeman, student, cook or business man, but if you are doing that in disobedience to God's will for your life then you are in unbelief. You are going to be a very unhappy and disappointed Christian until you repent and get back in faith. Make up your heart and mind that no matter how difficult it may feel you are going to do what God has called you to do. You are going to trust the Lord to provide everything you need, to open up every door and to clear the way before you; despite what the devil or people say! If we (Christians) will operate in the kind of determined faith Jesus did, then we will see and experience the same results (Mark 16:17-20; John 14:12-14)!!

Matthew 14:22-32 says:

"Immediately Jesus made His disciples get into the boat and go before Him to the other side, while He sent the multitudes away.

And when He had sent the multitudes away, He went up on the mountain by Himself to pray. Now when evening came, He was alone there.

But the boat was now in the middle of the sea, tossed by the waves, for the wind was contrary.

Now in the fourth watch of the night Jesus went to them, walking on the sea,

And when the disciples saw Him walking on the sea, they were troubled, saying, "It is a ghost!" And they cried out for fear,

But immediately Jesus spoke to them, saying, "Be of good cheer! It is I; do not be afraid,"

And Peter answered Him and said, "Lord, if it is You, command me to come to You on the water."

So He said, "Come." And when Peter had come down out of the boat, he walked on the water to go to Jesus,

But when he saw that the wind was boisterous, he was afraid; and beginning to sink he cried out,

saying, "Lord, save me!"

And immediately Jesus stretched out His hand and caught him, and said to him, "O you of little faith, why did you doubt?"

And when they got into the boat, the wind ceased."

Let's look at some important things here. Jesus was on the mountain praying while his disciples were in a boat being tossed by the waves. Then He goes to them walking on the water. In my mind's eye, I like to picture how I see Jesus walking to them on the water. I see Him walking down the mountain to the water's edge and without making any change in His stride, continue walking out onto the water. When He went from land to water, He didn't hesitate for a second! Then, I pause and imagine how most Christians would have done that. They would have had an awesome time praying on the mountain. Enjoying God's glory and presence, and feeling like their faith can move mountains. As they headed down to the water's edge, they would have walked with a spring in their steps. Upon approaching the end of land, their speed would quickly decelerate to a halt at the beginning of water (major mistake!). They would then proceed to put their foot on top of the water, apply a little weight, to see if it would hold them up, or get really dramatic (thinking they are stirring up their faith), ask someone to play the "alleluia chorus" and begin to scream to God saying, "Oh God in Heaven! You parted the red sea! You created the worlds in the beginning…!" They would go on and on, thinking their loudness and many words would cause their faith to soar. This phony spiritual façade would not get them back into faith. They got out the moment they hesitated at the water's edge.

One thing I've learned over the years is when the Lord tells you to do something, don't hesitate, obey immediately. I (and probably you) have missed it many times when the Lord wanted me to walk out on the water of life, to walk in victory over a situation or to minister to a person right then, and I didn't do it. I hesitated. I stopped and thought about it. I don't believe Jesus did that when He got to the water. He just kept on walking, as if it was dry land under His feet. The Lord wants to train us to do the same thing in our everyday lives. I heard one minister say that if you put on your bathing suit to walk across your pool, you are already defeated. Don't plan for defeat! Of course, make sure you've heard from God, then step out boldly in faith and start walking!

I believe the Lord is teaching His Church to live (and flow) in the supernatural realm just as normally as we live in the natural realm.

According to what we read in the four Gospels, Jesus did not put on a dramatic religious show when

He ministered to people. He flowed back and forth from the natural to the supernatural like breathing. All of us should ask ourselves this question, "What is normal Christianity?" Some time ago when I was studying the Word, God got me thinking about the word "marvel", what made Jesus marvel and what made the people marvel. There shouldn't be a difference but there was. In the dictionary, this word means something that evokes surprise, admiration, wonder, strong surprise or astonishment.

Matthew 9: 32,33 says: **"As they went out, behold, they brought to Him a man, mute and demon-possessed. And when the demon was cast out, the mute spoke, And the multitudes <u>marveled</u>, saying, "It was never seen like this in Israel!"**

In Matthew 8:27, after Jesus stopped the storm, it says, **So the men <u>marveled</u>, saying, "Who can this be, that even the winds and the sea obey Him?"** They marveled, were surprised when people were healed, demons were cast out and miracles were manifested; but that's not what Jesus marveled at.

Look at Mark 6:5,6.

"Now He could do no mighty work there, except that He laid His hands on a few sick people and healed them,

And He <u>marveled</u> because of their unbelief. Then He went about the villages in a circuit, teaching."

What surprised and astonished Jesus was the people's unbelief! The Bible <u>never</u> says that Jesus marveled when someone got healed or delivered, but the people did. Now, Jesus did marvel at the centurion's <u>great faith </u>in Matthew 8:10. That seemed to surprise Him because He wasn't use to seeing that in the people.

I believe what God considers normal Christianity would seem almost foreign to most Christians. We have been living far below our privileges in Christ. It's time we find out who we are in Him and start acting like it! Jesus was our example, let's pattern ourselves after Him. The four Gospels never describe Jesus being surprised when someone got healed. He expected it and was use to it. The Lord wants to use us so much that we get use to it, so to speak. To be use to it doesn't mean we are not excited, but we're not surprised either, because we know our God. When I touch the power button on my television, I'm not surprised when the picture comes on, because I'm use to it. I'm still glad (excited) though, but it's not because that's the first time I've ever seen the television come on. I don't marvel that it came on, that's what I expected.

Look at something else the Lord brought to my attention in the story we read of Jesus walking on the water. In Matthew 14:26, it says, **"And when the disciples saw Him walking on the sea, they were troubled, saying, "It is a <u>ghost</u>!" And they cried out for fear."**

The Lord was out there walking on the water. A man was walking on the water! They couldn't believe a man could be walking on the water. That wasn't *normal* to them, so their mind reasoned that it had to be a ghost (spirit). Only a spirit of some kind would not sink in the water. One of the main reasons there are so many cults and false religions in the world is because of the church. Yes, you heard me right, because of all of us (Christians).

Our lack of continuing Jesus' ministry has resulted in the rapid growth of false teachings throughout the world. When ministers water down God's Word (II Corinthians 2:17) and won't proclaim it uncompromisingly in love, they give the devil greater place to promote his agenda! We haven't been walking in the fullness of what God called us to do and we must get back to it! If you are ministering to someone and God gives you a word of knowledge about them (something you don't know on your own, supernaturally revealed to you) and they respond by saying that you are psychic; that's a sure sign that we haven't been demonstrating God's Kingdom enough.

The Lord wants to use all believers in doing the works Jesus did and greater works- in church, at work, in the market place and everywhere we go, so much, that when a believer calls out a supernatural word from God, the people will say that you must be a Christian. When they hear of someone walking on the water, being healed or receiving a miracle, the first words out of their mouths should be, "that must be one of those Christians. You know they do that all the time." God wants to use us more than we can imagine in continuing Jesus' ministry on this earth and demonstrating that He is the True and only God, all powerful and perfect love. If we would yield to His Spirit in us and let Him have His way through us, then less people would be pulled into the morass of the deception and lies of cults and false religions. The Lord created a hunger in all human beings for the supernatural, but we must reach them first with God's supernatural. The Lord is raising up a mighty spiritual army, His church. It may look like a remnant, but it's growing rapidly! Let us make sure that we're right in the center of it!

Think about Peter stepping out of the boat and walking on the water, a man, not a ghost. Matthew 14:29-31 says,

"So He said, "Come." And when Peter had come down out of the boat, he walked on the water

to go to Jesus.

But when he saw that the wind was boisterous, he was afraid; and beginning to sink he cried out, saying, "Lord, save me!"

And immediately Jesus stretched out His hand and caught him, and said to him, "O you of little faith, why did you doubt?"

Peter actually walked on the water. It didn't say that he stepped out and was moving his legs, as if to walk, while really sinking. The Bible says that <u>he walked </u>on the water and didn't begin to sink until he took his eyes off Jesus (the Word) and looked at his circumstances. What an awesome miracle for Peter! You know his heart was pounding with joy and excitement! He's the only man (besides Jesus) we have on record, in the Bible, that walked on water. Even though he began to sink and Jesus saved him, you know he was still thrilled! What happened next was probably a major shock to his system! Jesus rebuked him! Even though he was the <u>only</u> one who got out of the boat and walked on the water, He still rebuked him. Why?

If that had been any of us today, we would have been complimenting and praising him for his great courage to step out of the boat. We would have said to Peter, "You are the only one who walked on the water. The other disciples didn't even try to operate in faith. You may have sunk a little, but you still walked on water. We are so proud of you!" Now, either we would have missed it in what we said, or Jesus missed it. Remember, Jesus was training His disciples in how to <u>live</u> (every day) by faith. He wasn't training them so they could have only **one** testimony for the rest of their lives. If that's all that Peter ever did, he would have something wonderful to tell his kids and grandkids, but that wasn't what the Lord had in mind. God doesn't want us to see our faith work one time and that's it. He knows we are going to make mistakes. He knows there will be times we miss it, but thank God for His infinite mercy. Don't be satisfied with one successful faith endeavor and then quit.

The reason the Lord spoke to Peter so strongly was to arrest his attention to this very fact. He wanted him to know that this wasn't just a one time event but a life lesson. How he responded to Jesus saying, "come" could affect the rest of his life and ministry. The very fact that He rebuked him meant that he <u>didn't</u> have to fail. If the Lord knows He can't expect us to operate in faith more than one or two times then He would not have rebuked Peter. He would be glad for any amount of fruit we bore for His Kingdom, without encouraging us to produce more. What happened to Peter is evidence to me that the Lord expects a lot more out of us every day. His experience on the water motivates us to keep stepping out in faith and obeying God, knowing each day we will walk farther and farther on the water of life without sinking!

In Mark chapter 4, a similar situation happened to all the disciples, verses 35-40 says:

On the same day, when evening had come, He said to them, "Let us cross over to the other side."

Now when they had left the multitude, they took Him along in the boat as He was. And other little boats were also with Him.

And a great windstorm arose, and the waves beat into the boat, so that it was already filling.

But He was in the stern, asleep on a pillow. And they awoke Him and said to Him, "Teacher, do You not care that we are perishing?"

Then He arose and rebuked the wind, and said to the sea, "Peace, be still!" And the wind ceased and there was a great calm.

But he said to them, "Why are you so fearful? How is it that you have no faith?"

Jesus spoke the command of faith when He said, "Let us cross over to the other side." He didn't say they would go half way and sink. He believed what He said would come to pass, and then took a nap. One of the main ways to know you're in faith is if you're in peace. Some Christians have a good confession, but they are not in faith because their hearts are filled with worry and fear. Your heart has to line up with your mouth. That's where all of us have missed it many times. What you are going through may seem like a fiery furnace, but if you are truly in faith, you'll have perfect peace in the middle of it!

Remember the devil can manipulate things in the natural realm, and that's what he did in this situation. I pray that the Lord will brand in your mind what I'm about to say. The devil <u>cannot</u> stop your faith from working! His only strategy is to convince you, by what you see, feel and hear that it's not working. He <u>cannot</u> turn your faith off, only you can! He hopes you'll never find that out. The devil stirs up the circumstances expecting you to say something like, "I guess it didn't work. I guess I didn't get my healing, I still feel pain. I guess the money isn't coming in." Jesus knew that despite the seriousness of the storm, they were going to the other side. He wasn't going to change what he believed or said. The problem was, the disciples didn't know that. After they woke Him up, He demonstrated how to operate in faith by stopping the storm then He rebuked them. He said, "Why don't you have any faith?" In Luke's account, He said, "Where's your faith?" Now you know they were probably terrified by this storm.

They were in a boat, but it wasn't one of the big cruise liners we have today. Yet, He jumped all over them. He didn't try to comfort them. If that had been anybody but Jesus who talked that way to those men, he would have been reprimanded for it. Most of our church leaders would have said, "How could you talk that way to these men. They've been traumatized. Don't you know how to walk in love? You have a lot of growing to do." Or they would have walked over to the disciples, put their arms around them and said, "Let's have a group hug. I know that was a scary storm and I was afraid myself. It's perfectly understandable to react the way you did, maybe next time you'll do better." Think about this with me. If Jesus had not been there, they would have died! They didn't need a group hug. They didn't need to be patted on the back and told, "It's ok". They needed guidance from someone like a drill sergeant, who knows if you don't get this right it could cost you your life!

Some Christians think learning to live by faith is so they can get all the "things" they want, but it's much more than that. We have an enemy (the devil) out there and everyday he's planning ways to attack and remove us from this earth, so we better get 100% committed to God and quit playing church! Ephesians 6:16 says our shield of *faith* will quench <u>all</u>

the fiery darts of the wicked one, but that's contingent upon keeping our shield of faith activated.

God is very serious about His children learning how to live a supernatural lifestyle, to use their faith every day, and not to be a "one hit wonder". He wants us to be just as successful in <u>living</u> by faith and in ministering to others, as Jesus was! I didn't say that we are there yet, but let's keep pressing in to be all God wants us to be!

2

THE KEY

While out witnessing again in Dallas, Chris, I and two other students from the Bible school parked our car in front of the Spot Light Bar. After we got out of the car, we began talking to a pimp named Wine. He was standing right in front of the bar. While we were telling him about Jesus, a drunk man came out and walked over to us. He asked us what we were talking about. Chris said that we were talking about Jesus and asked, "Do you believe in Him?" The man said, "oh yea!" Chris asked again, "Is Jesus the Lord of your life?" He responded, "oh yea! Sure!" He was almost falling down drunk, so we knew he didn't know what he was saying. Then, he looked over at Wine and asked him if he believed in this "Jesus". Wine took about 20 seconds of silence before telling the man "not really". Let me remind you, if you've been around drunk people they say a lot of dumb things and repeat themselves. The drunk man then said to Wine "I just live down the road. I have two cars at my house, and if you'll believe what they're telling you about this Jesus, I'll give you one." Quickly, Wine said, "I believe it! Where do you live?" He repeated once more, "I just live down this road and if you will believe what they are telling you about Jesus, I will give one of my cars." Again, Wine answered, "I told you that I believe! Where do you live?" Sometimes it seems like drunk people go deaf, because he acted like he never heard his answer. Then, to all our surprise, the drunk (and crazy) guy pulled this steel object out of his pocket and pointed it right in Wine's face; almost touching his nose. It was made of steel and had a trigger in the middle. The drunk guy said very sternly to him, "this is a homemade 22 Pistol and if you don't believe what these people are saying, I'm going to blow your head off!" Well, you have never heard someone "seemingly" believe God so fast in your life! Wine tried his very best to convince that man that he was a Christian, loved Jesus and was all for God. We knew he was lying through his teeth, but he didn't want to die.

All of a sudden, the man pulls the gun down and starts to walk away. I thought he was leaving. I motioned to Chris and said that we should head back to the Bible school (I think we all had enough for one night). I had just gotten in the driver's side when the drunk guy came back with his gun. He came over to the passenger side, opened the door, put the gun in his left hand, stuck his head in the car at me, held the gun to the temple of the right side of my head and said, "I want a ride!" While holding the gun there, he pulled his head out of the car and starts looking around (demons make people crazy). That's why my first thought was that I might be able to grab his gun with my right hand, since he wasn't looking. But, just as quickly as that thought came, I dismissed it, because if that didn't work I would have a bullet in my head. Then I got back in faith, I decided to use Jesus Name and come against the devil that was operating through him.

I don't know if the man heard this but I know the devil did. While looking out my windshield, with a strong voice I said, "Satan, I bind you in Jesus' Name and I command you to stop in your maneuvers against me right now!" The instant I finished making that command, the man looked back in the car at me, pulled the gun away from my head and threw it in the air towards the front of the bar. He then closed my passenger door and walked off down the highway into the dark. We never saw him again. We picked up the gun, and by what we could tell, it was a real homemade pistol. Praise the Lord for His protection! There is all power in Jesus Name! I learned something that night about the Name of Jesus and how much His name belongs to us. There's salvation, healing, prosperity, deliverance and of course protection in Jesus' Name! His Name is truly a strong tower that we can run into and be safe (Proverbs 18:10)!

John 14:12-14

"Most assuredly, I say to you, he who believes in Me, the works that I do he will do also; and greater works than these he will do, because I go to My Father.

And whatever you ask in My name, that I will do, that the Father may be glorified in the Son.

If you ask anything in My name, I will do it."

John 16:23

"And in that day you will ask Me nothing. Most assuredly, I say to you, whatever you ask the Father in My name He will give you."

The Lord Jesus authorized all believers (those who believe in Him as their personal Lord and Savior- Romans 10:9) to use His Name. He is all powerful. He and His Name are one; therefore His Name is all powerful!

By telling us that we can do the works He did and greater works in His Name, He's authorizing us to use

His Name. By being authorized to use His name, we have the legal right to use all of the power, dominion and resources in His Name! We are authorized ones! I like to confess that I am an authorized one! The Name of Jesus belongs to <u>you</u> just as much as it does to Jesus! Remember, we are His body (I Corinthians 12:13; Ephesians 1:22,23; Colossians 1:18). He is the head. His head and body are like ours, they're connected. Think about this with me. My name "Dwayne" belongs to my body as much as it does to my head. My name belongs to my knee, toe, arm, hand, shoulders, etc. just as much as it belongs to my head. If my knees could talk, they would have the authority or right to use all that's in my name. Well, the same is true for Jesus and His body.

You and I have the right to use all of God's unlimited power in His Name to do the same works He did and even greater works! He said so, we just read it. Let's get busy using His Name to expand His Kingdom and to glorify the Father in the Son!

If you haven't seen this before, it's important that you understand the difference in what Jesus is saying in John 14 and John 16. In John 14, the Lord is talking about using His Name more in spiritual warfare by commanding the devil's works to be destroyed, like I did when the man held the gun on my head. I didn't pray to the Father. I spoke to the devil in Jesus' Name and told him to stop! He had to obey me because all of God's power was available to me (in the Name) to stop him! <u>You</u> have the same Name and the same rights! God did everything for us through Jesus' shed Blood, death and resurrection! Let's take advantage of our rights and privileges! Resist the devil! Resist everything he's bringing against you and he <u>will</u> flee from you (James 4:7)!! Now, in John 16, the Lord is talking about using His Name in prayer. He said to ask the Father in His Name. So when we pray, we don't pray to Jesus or the Holy Spirit. We pray to our Father in the Name of Jesus. But, when the devil brings sickness, fear, lack, lust, doubt, and any of his curse against us, we speak to it and command it to leave us in Jesus Name! It <u>must</u> obey because we are the **authorized** ones!

Let me remind you that the New Testament was mainly written in Greek. The word "ask" that we read in these verses in the book of John is the same Greek word, but it has several meanings and it's used differently in both of John's references. According to the Strong's Exhaustive Concordance, number 154 & 4441, this word means: to **ask, beg, call for, crave, desire, require** and also, **a demand of something due**.

In John 16:23, Jesus told us <u>not</u> to *ask* Him anything, but to ask the Father in His Name. Yet, in chapter 14, He said that we could *ask* Him anything in His Name. The Lord wasn't contradicting Himself.

He knew that we could use His Name in prayer to the Father as well as in spiritual warfare where you command and demand the devil (directly-like Jesus did) to take his hands off of people, situations, governments, cities and churches.

Let me paraphrase John 14:12-14. The Lord was saying that whatever you command (not commanding Jesus) to be done in My Name, I <u>will</u> do it! When you demand sickness to die and demons to leave in My Name, I <u>will</u> do it! When you command the devil to take his hands off of your marriage, children and finances in My Name, I <u>will</u> do it! He didn't say that He might do it. He said that He <u>will</u> do it! No one and nothing can stop Jesus from bringing to pass what He said He would do!! He will use all of His power on our behalf because we are **authorized!**

Peter and John understood this about Jesus Name. They understood what Jesus meant in John 14:12-14. They knew the difference in using Jesus Name to *speak* the command of faith verses *praying* (to the Father) the prayer of faith.

Acts 3:1-8,16 says:

"Now Peter and John went up together to the temple at the hour of prayer, the ninth hour.

And a certain man lame from his mother's womb was carried, whom they laid daily at the gate of the temple which is called Beautiful, to ask

alms from those who entered the temple;

Who, seeing Peter and John about to go into the temple, asked for alms.

And fixing his eyes on him, with John, Peter said, "Look at us."

So he gave them his attention, expecting to receive something from them.

Then Peter said, "Silver and gold I do not have, but what I do have I give you: In the name of Jesus Christ of Nazareth, rise up and walk."

And he took him by the right hand and lifted him up, and immediately his feet and ankle bones receive strength.

So he, leaping up, stood and walked and entered the temple with them-walking, leaping, and praising God.

And His name, through faith in His name, has made this man strong, whom you see and know. Yes, the faith which comes through Him has given him this perfect soundness in the presence of you all."

The Apostle Peter said that the man was healed because of *faith* in Jesus Name. In verse 12, he said that the man wasn't healed because of their power or godliness. In other words, it wasn't because of them personally. You don't have to be perfect to use Jesus Name. You just have to <u>believe</u> in His Name.

Again, the Lord helped me to understand this back around 1980. I was about 23 years old. I was working for Dr. Norvel Hayes in his Campus Challenge Ministry. Brother Norvel sent teams of young people out to the big college campuses to witness to the students, but we also had a job so we could make a little money. We worked for one of his businesses called Varsity Engravers. During the day we would sell personalized stationary in the fraternity and sorority houses to pay for our food and expenses then we would go out witnessing. We usually did not make enough to pay for a hotel so we would call pastors of churches that believed in brother Norvel's ministry to see if they knew any one we could stay with for a couple of weeks. When we came to work the university in upper Ohio, we thought it would be good to stay in the Columbus area. So, I called pastor Rod Parsley and asked if he knew anyone we could stay with. Without hesitation, he said that we could stay with him. He wasn't married then and his church was just getting started. One evening in his home, I, my partner Ron, pastor Parsley's mother and sister were sitting in the living room talking (pastor Rod might have been over at his church). They told us that pastor Rod's sister had already experienced 70 strokes. The devil tried to kill her 70 times and did not succeed, Praise the Lord. His sister was sitting right in front of me talking with us. She seemed perfectly fine. I asked pastor Rod's mother if I could use their phone to call my parents in Florida. The phone wasn't too far behind his sister. I got up, walked over and picked up the phone and began to dial the number. While the phone was ringing I noticed something strange happening to his sister. Her eyes seemed to roll back into her head, it looked as if her tongue stuck to the roof of her mouth and she quit breathing. Then her arms fell off the arm rest. The Lord spoke to me (not audibly, but in my heart) and said, "I want you to cast the spirit of death out of her!" I hung up the phone, walked over to her and very strongly commanded the spirit of death to come out of her in Jesus' Name!

As soon as I said that her mouth opened and she began to breathe normally! She sat up straight, began to move around and acted like nothing had happened. Completely free!

The Lord saved her that night, and gave me a greater revelation of the power in Jesus Name. The Name didn't work for me because of my good works. I learned that you don't have to be in the ministry for 50 years or know everything about the Bible for the Name to work for you. You just need to have faith *in* the Name. I didn't say that you had to have faith to *use* the Name. There's a very important difference. Here's something I learned from Kenneth Hagin Sr. years ago. The Lord Jesus taught him that the Name of Jesus is like having a key to something. The key will unlock what it goes to. If you have the key, you are considered the authorized one. For example, I have a key to my car. The key to my car will turn it on so I can drive it. I have faith *in* my key. I believe in what it can do. I believe that it can start my car. Now, here's what I want you to see. I don't need faith to *use* my key. Do you see it? <u>My</u> key belongs to me. I don't have to have faith to use what is mine. If I asked my wife to pray that I would have faith to use my car key, she would think that something is wrong with my mind. She would probably want to pray for my head. It's just good common sense, and most everyone knows if something belongs to you then you don't need faith to use it. You just use it! You have the right to use it whenever you want to because it's yours! Again, the Name of Jesus belongs to you (every Christian)! You don't need faith to *use* the Name, but you <u>must</u> have faith *in* the Name. You don't have to have a degree in theology or be a Bible scholar! But, you do need to believe *in* what Jesus Name can do. Faith *in* His Name comes by hearing the Word about His Name (Romans 10:17). Get the Scriptures out of this book and all of the rest in the Bible and start reading, meditating and confessing them, and God will build your faith *in* Jesus' Name.

Acts 4:7-10 says:

"And when they had set them in the midst, they asked, "By what power or by what name have you done this?"

Then Peter, filled with the Holy Spirit, said to them, "Rulers of the people and elders of Israel:

"If we this day are judged for a good deed done to a helpless man, by what means he has been made well,

"let it be known to you all, and to all the people of Israel, that by <u>the name</u> of Jesus Christ of Nazareth, whom you crucified, whom God raised from the dead, <u>by Him</u> this man stands here before you whole."

Even the religious leaders recognized that it was the power in Jesus' Name that healed the man. To some degree, they had faith in the power of a name. They understood that a person's name represented who they are and all they're abilities. They knew if you could use (or be authorized) another person's name who was very wealthy and powerful it would be the same as having that person (physically) there with you. People would show you the same respect they would show the wealthy person, just because you have the right to use their name. If you look at verse 10 again, Peter said that the man was healed by the Name or by Him (Jesus). Do you see that? Peter was saying that when you have the Name of Jesus, it's just the same as having Jesus! Wow! We don't need Jesus to appear in the flesh and walk around with us everywhere we go. We have His Name (the key)! Plus, we know He lives in us through the Holy Spirit whom God has given us. Is it any wonder why the 70 disciples were so excited when they returned to Jesus, in Luke 10:17, and said, **"Lord, even the demons are subject to us in Your name."** Why? Because Jesus' Name is the Name above all names!

Philippians 2:9-11 says:

"Therefore God also has highly exalted Him and give Him the name which is above every name,

that at the name of Jesus every knee should bow, of those in heaven, and of those on earth, and of those under the earth,

and that every tongue should confess that Jesus Christ is Lord, to the glory of God the Father."

The Name that God has given us is higher than the names of every being and everything in Heaven, Earth and Hell! Whoever has the most exalted and greatest name has the most power. The devil, demons, sickness, poverty, sin, fear, doubt and everything in the kingdom of darkness has a name, but it has to submit and bow its knee to Jesus' Name! Therefore, whoever is authorized to use Jesus' Name will have all power and dominion over all of the works of the devil! It doesn't matter what the devil tries to bring against us as we preach the Gospel. We have The Name! Take out your key and use it! Keys unlock things! Use the Name of Jesus and unlock the chains of disease, poverty and fear in people's lives! You have the key that can set them free! I hope you will use it! You know, the key to my car won't do me any good if I leave it on the table in my house. I have to use it before I can experience the ability and power of that key. I believe the Great Commission will mean more to you now.

Mark 16:17,18 says:

"And these signs will follow those who believe: <u>In My name</u> they will cast out demons; they will speak with new tongues, they will take up serpents; and if they drink anything deadly, it will by no means hurt them; they will lay hands on the sick, and they will recover."

The demon doesn't come out just because you <u>have</u> the key. My car doesn't start just because I <u>have</u> the key to it. It starts when I use my key. When I'm ministering to a person being attacked by a demon, I command it to leave in Jesus' Name! The example we have of taking up serpents is found in Acts 28, where Paul was bit by a snake. He wasn't testing the

Lord by trying to pick them up on purpose, so let's not stretch it past the only Biblical example that we have! He didn't know that was going to happen to him, but when it did, he shook it off! He knew in Jesus' Name that he could "take up" serpents. He didn't just "carry" the Name of Jesus around with him. He boldly used that wonderful Name to preach the Gospel and demonstrate God's Kingdom in Spirit and power! Mighty signs and wonders were manifested everywhere he went! We must expect the same results! We are authorized to use the same key! Let's start unlocking the doors and setting the captives free!

3

YOU GIVE THEM SOMETHING TO EAT

Are we (the church) continuing Jesus ministry on the earth? Are we ministering to people like Jesus did? Are we teaching, preaching, healing the sick and casting out demons in our churches and everywhere we go? Has anyone mistaken us for "gods" as they did Paul and Barnabas at Lystra in Acts 14?

Matthew 14:15-21 says:

"When it was evening, His disciples came to Him, saying, "This is a deserted place, and the hour is already late. Send the multitudes away, that they may go into the villages and buy themselves food."

But Jesus said to them, "They do not need to go away. <u>You give them something to eat</u>."

And they said to Him, "We have here only five

loaves and two fish."

He said, "Bring them here to Me."

Then He commanded the multitudes to sit down on the grass. And He took the five loaves and the two fish, and looking up to heaven, He blessed and broke and gave the loaves to the disciples; and the disciples gave to the multitudes.

So they all ate and were filled, and they took up twelve baskets full of the fragments that remained.

Now those who had eaten were about five thousand men, besides women and children."

The Bible says that they were in a deserted place and that 5,000 men were there. It didn't say this was only a men's meeting. Well, if you have 5,000 men, you will have women and children as well. It's very reasonable to assume that there was at least 10,000 or more people gathered together to hear Jesus that day.

The disciples came to Jesus and told him that the people were hungry and He needed to send them home to get food, but I want you to pay close attention to what Jesus told <u>them</u>. He said, "<u>you</u> give them something to eat." Obviously, by their response, they didn't understand what He said. Their answer was, "We only have five loaves and two fish." Most of us would have given Him the same answer. You may even be puzzled right now at what I'm talking about. You see, they were thinking in the natural realm. Jesus was thinking in the supernatural realm. They were thinking about what they could do in the flesh or by their own efforts, without God's intervention. He was thinking that all things are possible to him who believes (Mark 9:23). Listen to this! Jesus was actually telling them, you need to use your faith in God and work a miracle for these people! I want (you!) to feed them. Jesus went on to do it, but he expected them to.

Whenever I meditate the Word, I like to imagine myself in the disciples place and the Lord giving me that command. How would I respond to it? If I had some of the understanding I do now, I would remind myself of this very important truth. The Lord would never command me to do something that I could not do; no matter how impossible it looked. The very fact that He told me to do it, meant He must have given me the ability, faith, anointing or whatever I needed to do it. Think about that. Jesus told them to feed probably 10,000 or more people. He meant, "I want you to work a miracle for them!"

Now, as soon as you say something like that, the religious people (those who have a form of godliness, but deny its power-II Timothy 3:5) will speak up. They'll say, "Remember, we can't do anything by ourselves. We are nothing without Jesus." I agree with that 100%! We can't do anything apart from the Lord Jesus. Without Christ, our righteousness is as filthy rags. We couldn't heal a sick gnat by ourselves. We have no power, faith or abilities apart from the Holy Spirit. But! We are not by ourselves anymore! Yes, we don't want to ever forget that we depend totally on Jesus for everything! Listen! This is one of the areas where the devil has deceived many Christians. They think they have to constantly remind themselves of who they are without Christ to stay humble, but just the opposite is true. We are not without Christ anymore! He lives in us and we live in Him! We are His body and He is our head! We are one spirit with Him (I Corinthians 6:17)! We are seated in Him at the Father's right hand in the Heavenly places (Ephesians 2:5,6)! Right now are we sons of God (I John 3:2)! Like the world says, "don't deny who you are!" It time for the REAL church to stand up and act like God's mighty sons and daughters on the earth!! Paul told us, in Philemon 6, that we need to acknowledge or declare every good thing in us in Christ! The more I confess how great Jesus is in me and who I am in Him, the more I'm reminded that without Him I can do nothing. If you want to truly humble yourself under God's mighty hand then cast all of your cares on Him by acknowledging that He is your source and all your strength in Christ (I Peter 5:6,7)!

Jesus could have told his disciples, "God is going to feed them through you" but He didn't. He chose to say it the way He chose to say it. He knew exactly what He was doing. Whether the disciples fully realized it or not, they were always in training with Jesus. He wanted them and us today, to flow in God's supernatural realm as He did. They didn't follow Him around just to see the miracles, but to learn how to operate in faith and do the same works He did in His Name.

If you listen closely in your spirit, I believe you will hear the Lord say "You give them something to eat, you heal them, you speak to that mountain, you cast out the demon, you command the storm to stop, you feed the sheep, you do it in Jesus' Name!" When you step out in faith and obey God, it will be Jesus by the Holy Spirit through you who does all the works.

When my daughter was very young, before she went to high school, her mother took her to the doctor for a checkup. She told me when she got home that the doctor said her spine was crooked and she had scoliosis. He said she would probably have to wear a back brace all through high school. Her mother did through her high school years. When I heard that news I told my daughter we were not going to have that. We were not going to allow that to operate in her body. So, for the next 12 nights, after my daughter went to bed, I would go into her room and lay my hands on her back and speak to her spine. While she was sleeping, with my hands on her back, I would say, "Scoliosis, I curse you in Jesus' Name! I command you to get out of my daughter's back right now!   All of the bones, vertebrae, and disks, I command you to move into correct alignment the way God created you to be for a perfectly normal back in Jesus' Name!" I only did that for 12 nights because her mother took her back to the doctor again. This time my daughter had some great news. After the doctor checked her back, he said there was no scoliosis and her back was fine! Praise the Lord! She is now 24 years old, working on her Master's degree and has never worn a back brace. Jesus told you and me to feed the people in His Name! That means to heal the people! Deliver the people! Lead the people to Jesus! Bless the people! Be the vessel that God works through to bring miracles to the people!

Let me share something else very important about how Jesus ministered to the people. Did you know that He really <u>never</u> prayed for any individual person? I didn't say that He never took time to pray in His private life. We know that He might spend all night in prayer with the Father. The next time you read the four Gospels, pay close attention to every time He healed the sick, cast out demons, controlled the weather, etc.. He always spoke the command of faith. He would say, "Rise and walk, your faith has made you whole, come out of him, winds and sea be still, you are loosed from your infirmity, stretch out your hand, be cleansed, as you have believed-let it be done unto you, you give them something to eat, He said, "come" to Peter and he walked on the water, let us cross over to the other side, Lazarus come forth, let down your nets for a catch, He said, "man, your sins are forgiven you", be opened and he rebuked the fever in Peter's mother-n-law. In Mark 9:25, Jesus <u>rebuked</u> the unclean spirit. He didn't say, "Father, I pray that you will deliver this boy from this evil spirit." There is no Scripture where a sick person came to Jesus and He paused and prayed, "Father in Heaven, would you please heal this person?" He just said, "Be cleansed or be healed." And guess what? He was!

God has provided many ways for us to be healed and set free in His Word. They are all good. There is nothing wrong with acting on any of them, but I find it interesting that Jesus had only one main way that He ministered to people. He always decreed and commanded what He expected to come to pass. He always called those things which be not (manifested) as though they were (Romans 4:17). In John 9:6,7, Jesus made clay with His saliva, anointed the blind man's eyes and told him, "<u>Go, wash in the pool of Siloam</u>". Even though He used clay and saliva, there was still some type of declaration or command of faith. Jesus didn't anoint his eyes and then pray to the Father for healing. There is nothing wrong with that, but it's not the way the Spirit of God led Jesus to minister healing to the sick.

Please make sure you understood what I just said. I <u>did not</u> say that you cannot pray for the sick. James 5:14,15 tells us that the prayer of faith is one of the ways the sick can be healed. I just want you to see that Jesus never used that way. Just because He didn't use that way doesn't make it wrong. It's one of many Scriptural and valid ways the sick can be healed. Now, John 14:12-14, should be more real to us. Remember, Jesus said whatever we ask (command or demand to be done) in His Name, He will do it. He's our example, and He wants us to minister like He did. Obviously, if the Lord tells you a specific way to minister to someone, you need to do it that way, but we still need to understand that Jesus set a pattern for us, and we should follow it. I believe the Lord wants His church to get back to operating as kings and priests in Christ (Romans 5:17; Revelation 1:6; 5:10)! Kings decree things! We need to minister to people more through decreeing, declaring and prophesying things to be done in Jesus' Name (Job 22:28; Matthew 21:21; Mark 11:23)!!

I was reminded of the story when Jesus turned the water into wine. John 2:3,4 says:

"And when they ran out of wine, the mother of Jesus said to Him, "They have no wine."

Jesus said to her, "Woman, what does your concern have to do with me? My hour has not yet

come."

His mother said to the servants, "Whatever He says to you, do it."

When she said, "They have no wine", that was another way of saying, "You need to give them something to eat or You need to give them some wine." Jesus knew what that meant. He didn't do like His disciples and say, "where are we going to get enough money to buy wine for all these people?" He knew He needed to believe God for a miracle for these people. We know the rest of the story. He stepped out in faith and turned the water into wine.

If someone comes to you that's in pain it's fine to pray for them to be healed, but that's not the way Jesus would have done it. He would have spoken to the pain and commanded it to leave or told the person to be healed! It just seems to me, if we want to see the same results Jesus saw, we should follow His example. Jesus said that we are to speak to the mountain (which could be any problem or anything) and tell it to be removed and cast into the sea (Matthew 17:20; 21:21; Mark 11:23; Luke 17:6). He said if we believe in our heart what we say will come to pass then it will come to pass. Dr. Norvel Hayes always said that no one ever died of cancer that talked to it! I think a lot of Christians don't want to speak the command of faith to the sick person's body because it seems like it demands a more immediate response, and if the healing isn't manifested instantly, they are embarrassed. When you know Jesus is doing all the works <u>through you</u>, there's nothing for *you* to be embarrassed about. Jesus is the healer. You are just the vessel He's working through (II Corinthians 4:7).

So, if you have time, after ministering to a person, ask him or her if he can tell any difference in his body. Don't be afraid to ask him if he can tell any change in his physical condition. You won't mind asking him this question, if you are not concerned with how you look in front of the people. Your only desire should be to get the person healed. Remember, Jesus ministered to a blind man twice before his healing was fully manifested (Mark 8:22-25). If I have time I may lay hands on the person again. I may speak to his body again and remind it that this disease cannot live in it. All the rest of the pain has to go in Jesus' Name! Then, I'll ask him again if he can tell more of a difference in his body. Our goal is to see more instant healings and miracles in people's lives, but if they don't experience 100% manifestation immediately, let's believe God and work with them to get as close to that as we can. If I minister to someone who has pain in his leg, and 50% of it leaves; that's not a defeat, that's a victory. Even if they still feel half the pain, it's better than feeling all of it. Many times, after they leave, if they'll keep confessing in faith they're healed, the power of God will continue to work in their body and bring to pass the rest of their healing. It may all come to pass before they get home or a few days later. In Mark 16:17,18, Jesus said that Believers will lay hands on the sick and they (the sick) will (not might) recover. The word "recover" means to get back to a normal state. It doesn't always mean instantaneous. It implies that the person will get better in the process of time. We definitely need to expect more instant miracles and healings! But, if it doesn't happen immediately, I'm still thrilled it came to pass! God wants people healed and well, even if it not instantaneous.

As Christians, we need a greater reality that **we** are Christ's, His body! That <u>doesn't</u> mean we are Jesus. It <u>doesn't</u> mean we are Deity. Jesus is Jesus, but we are His body and one spirit with Him. We are His flesh and His bones on this earth (I Corinthians 3:23;6:17; II Corinthians 10:7; Ephesians 1:22,23;5:30; Colossians 1:18). Most of us, who believe God's Word, would agree with that, but it hasn't had a big enough impact upon our lives. Let me give you an example. Let's say it's about lunch time and you're getting really hungry. Your head tells your body to go to the store and get some food. Your body says, "Head, if you want some food, you get it." Would you be eating anything, anytime soon? It sounds a little silly doesn't it? No matter what your head wants, it will never get it if your body doesn't do something. Your head is subject to the obedience of your body.

Now, we don't have any problem with that when it comes to satisfying our flesh. But, when it comes to spreading the Gospel and stepping out in faith, we'll try to send the head to do it. You may be thinking, when have I done that? When the Lord tells you to witness to your neighbor and you refuse to. You'll say something like this, "if the Lord wants them saved, He (the Head) will save them. If the Lord wants my co-worker healed, He (the Head) will heal them." Yes, Jesus can appear to people in visions, but He's not carrying out the great commission apart from us. He told His body to go into all the world and preach the Gospel to every person. Jesus will save them through His body witnessing to them. Jesus will heal them through His body laying hands on them. If the body doesn't go, the job won't get done! If you say, "the Head will do it", no it won't! Your head will not go to the store and buy food for you, if your body refuses to leave the house. Do you see it? We truly are workers together with God (I Corinthians 3:9). I'm hoping this has given you a greater reality of how important you are to the work of the Lord. Every Believer counts! Every Believer is vital to God's will in Heaven being done on the earth

(Matthew 6:10)!

In the book of Acts, we see how the Believers understood they were the body of Christ and they continued ministering to people according to the pattern He gave them.

Acts 3:4,6 says:

"And fixing his eyes on him, with John, Peter said, "Look at us."

Then Peter said, "Silver and gold I do not have, but what I do have I give to you: <u>In the name of Jesus Christ of Nazareth, rise up and walk.</u>"

Peter said, "Look at us." Was he in pride? Did he not know that Jesus is the healer? Didn't he know (that by himself) he couldn't heal anyone? Peter knew exactly what he was doing. He knew he was the body, and the Head of the Church would heal the man through him. He also knew, if he didn't go to the temple and allow the Head to use His body, the man would not be healed. Also notice, that he didn't *pray* and ask the Father to heal the man. He imitated Jesus and <u>commanded</u> the man to rise and walk in Jesus' Name. Guess what? He did! He saw the same results Jesus saw.

Acts 9:33-35 says:

"There he found a certain man named Aeneas,

who had been bedridden eight years and was paralyzed.

And Peter said to him, "<u>Aeneas, Jesus the Christ heals you. Arise and make your bed.</u>" Then he arose immediately, so all who dwelt at Lydda and Sharon saw him and turned to the Lord."

He didn't pray for Aeneas. He didn't say, "Father would you please heal Aeneas of this condition?" There's nothing wrong with that. God answers prayers, but it's not the pattern Jesus (my example) gave us. I pray for leaders, nations, my church and family members, but when I minister to people, I put forth every effort to follow Jesus example. Look at the results of one demonstration of God's healing power! All the people in two towns got saved, Praise the Lord!

Acts 9:40,42 says:
"But Peter put them all out, and knelt down and prayed. And turning to the body he said, "<u>Tabitha, arise.</u>" And she opened her eyes, and when she saw Peter she sat up."

And it became known throughout all Joppa, and many believed on the Lord."

This verse says Peter prayed, then he spoke the

command of faith to her. He still followed the same pattern by ministering directly to her. Again, there is nothing wrong with praying. Sometimes, before I speak the command of faith to someone, I will pray first. I might pray in English or in tongues for direction from the Lord, to see if He will reveal something to me about this person or their situation. I want to know what to apply my faith for. Jesus many times would ask people what they wanted before He ministered to them. Again, look what happened! Through this awesome demonstration of God's Kingdom many were born-again (or believed in the Lord)!

Look how Saul (Paul) responded to Elymas the sorcerer in Acts 13:11,12.
"And now, indeed, the hand of the Lord is upon <u>you, and you shall be blind, not seeing the sun for a time."</u> And immediately a dark mist fell on him, and he went around seeking someone to lead him by the hand.
Then the proconsul believed, when he saw what had been done, being astonished at the teaching of the Lord."

He didn't pray and ask the Lord to make him blind. He was listening in his spirit, heard from the Lord and prophesied to the man what was about to happen to him. I believe Paul stayed in tune spiritually with the Lord by praying in tongues everywhere he went. The Holy Spirit edifies us when we pray in tongues or in the spirit (Jude 20). I Corinthians 14:14 says when we pray in tongues our spirit prays. Well, we are spirit beings. God created us in His image, He is spirit and He speaks to us in our spirits. So, the more we pray in tongues every day, the more in tune we will become to God's voice within.

Acts 14: 8-10 says:

"And in Lystra a certain man without strength in his feet was sitting, a cripple from his mother's womb, who had never walked.

This man heard Paul speaking. Paul, observing him intently and seeing that he had faith to be healed, said with a loud voice, "<u>Stand up straight on your feet!</u>" And he leaped and walked."

Paul could have prayed and said, "Lord, you can see this man has faith. Will you heal him now?" There's nothing Biblically incorrect about that prayer, but that's not the way the Spirit instructed Paul to minister healing to the man.

Acts 16: 16-18 says:

"Now it happened, as we went to prayer, that a certain slave girl possessed with a spirit of

divination met us, who brought her masters much profit by fortune-telling.

This girl followed Paul and us, and cried out, saying, "These men are the servants of the Most High God, who proclaim to us the way of salvation."

And this she did for many days. but Paul, greatly annoyed, turned and said to the spirit, "I command you in the name of Jesus Christ to come out of her." And he came out that very hour."

Paul didn't pray and ask the Lord to make the demon leave the girl. If he asked the Lord to do that, he would have asked the Head to do, what the body should do. God told <u>us</u> to resist the devil and he will flee (James 4:7). Jesus told <u>us</u> to cast out demons in His Name (Mark 16:17). Paul didn't speak to the girl, he spoke directly to the demon in her, told it to leave in Jesus' Name, and it did!

Acts 28: 8,9 says:

"And it happened that the father of Publius lay sick of a fever and dysentery. Paul went in to him and prayed, and he laid his hands on him and healed him.

so when this was done, the rest of those on the island who had diseases also came and were healed."

This seems similar to the time Peter ministered to Tabitha. Paul went into the man's "room" and prayed. I don't know what he prayed, but it may have been for instructions from the Lord, or he prayed in tongues a few minutes to edify himself in the Lord. Watch this closely. Then it says he laid his hands on him and (he) healed him. When it says "and healed him", it's implying that Paul healed him. Of course, we know Jesus did the healing through Paul, but remember, there are no hands in the Head. The Head needed His body to make his hands available, so the Head could send His power into the man. Will you make your hands and voice available so the Head can send His Word, Spirit and power through you to the people? **Will you give them something to eat**?

About the Author

Dwayne Norman is a 1978 graduate of Christ For The Nations Bible Institute in Dallas, Texas. He spent 3 years witnessing to prostitutes and pimps in the red light district of Dallas, and another 3 years ministering as a team leader in the Campus Challenge ministry of Dr. Norvel Hayes. He was ordained by Pastor Buddy and Pat Harrison of Faith Christian Fellowship in Tulsa, Oklahoma in September 1980, and is part of Dr. Ed Dufresne's Fresh Oil Fellowship. He also taught evangelism classes several times at Dr. Hayes' Bible school in Tennessee.

Soon the Lord led him to go on the road ministering. He ministers powerfully on soul winning, and on how God wants to use all Believers in demonstrating His Kingdom not just in Word but also in Power!

He teaches with clarity, the work that God accomplished for all believers in Christ from the cross to the throne, and the importance of this revelation to the church for the fulfillment of Jesus' commission to make disciples of all nations.

He strongly believes that we are called to do the works Jesus did and greater works in His Name, not just in church but especially in the market place. As a result Dwayne experiences many healing miracles in his services, arms and legs growing out, as well as other miracles.

He and his wife Leia travel and teach Supernatural Evangelism and train Believers in who they are in Christ and how to operate in their ministries.

To Inquire For Meetings With Dwayne & Leia Norman, Please contact them at:

Dwayne & Leia Norman
124 Evergreen Court
Mt. Sterling, KY 40353

(859) 351-6496
dwayne7@att.net
Web: www.dwaynenormanministries.org

Contact Dwayne to order his other books and products:

The Mystery DVD's (12 hours)	$50.00
The Mystery (book)	$12.00
The Mystery Study Guide (book)	$10.00
The Awesome Power in the Message of the Cross (book)	$10.00
Your Beginning with God (book)	$10.00
The Law of the Spirit of Life in Christ Jesus (book)	$10.00
Demonstrating God's Kingdom (book)	$10.00